FIRST 50 BAROQUE PIECES

YOU SHOULD PLAY ON THE PIANO

T0081865

ISBN 978-1-5400-4931-5

Copyright © 2019 by HAL LEONARD LLC
International Copyright Secured   All Rights Reserved

Visit Hal Leonard Online at
www.halleonard.com

Contact us:
Hal Leonard
7777 West Bluemound Road
Milwaukee, WI 53213
Email: info@halleonard.com

In Europe, contact:
Hal Leonard Europe Limited
42 Wigmore Street
Marylebone, London, W1U 2RN
Email: info@halleonardeurope.com

In Australia, contact:
Hal Leonard Australia Pty. Ltd.
4 Lentara Court
Cheltenham, Victoria, 3192 Australia
Email: info@halleonard.com.au

ADAGIO CON ESPRESSIONE
(Sarabande)

By JOHANN JACOB DE NEUFVILLE
(1759–1821)

Adagio con espressione

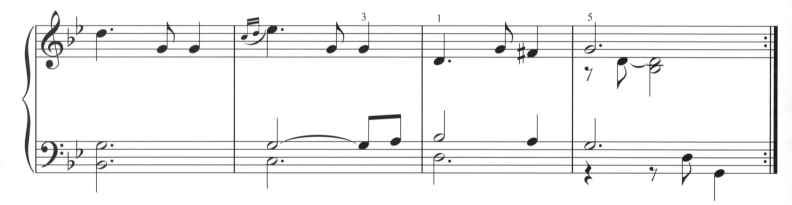

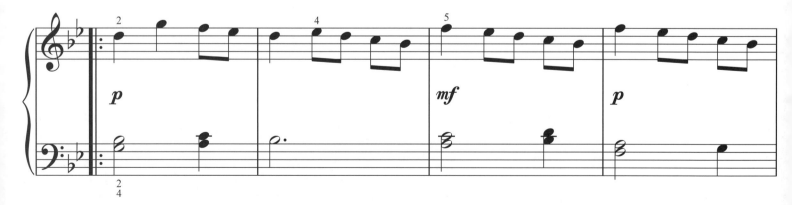

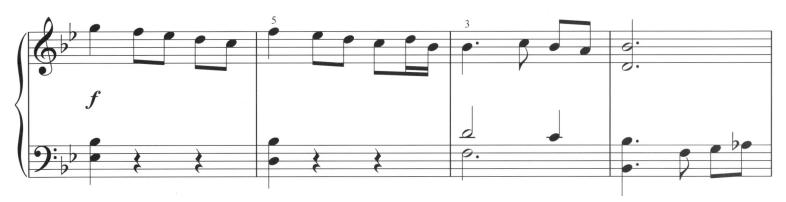

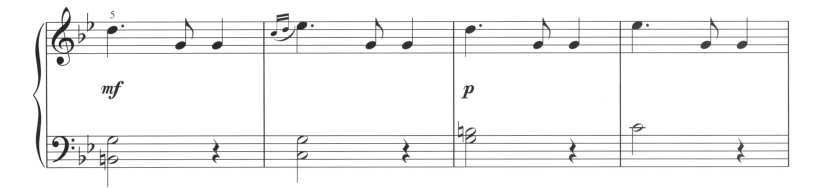

AIR
from WATER MUSIC

By GEORGE FRIDERIC HANDEL
(1685–1759)

Stately, in 2

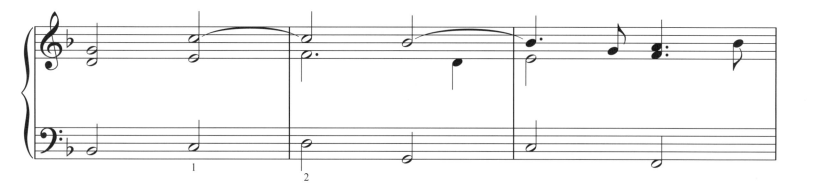

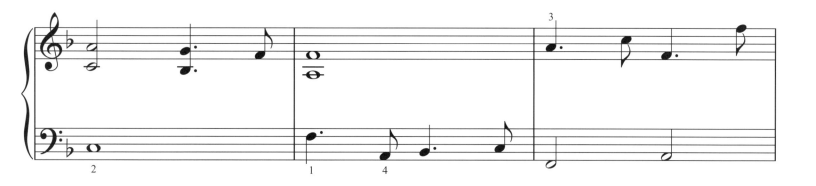

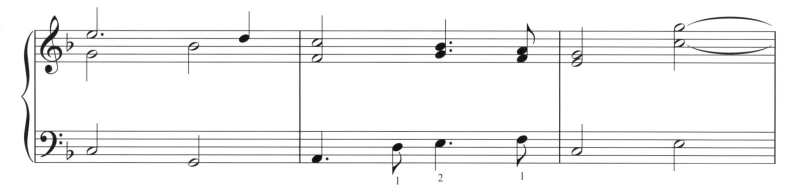

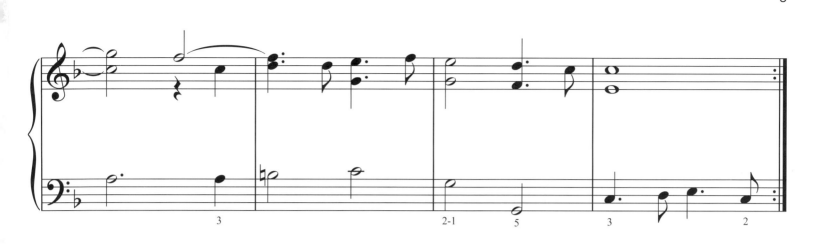

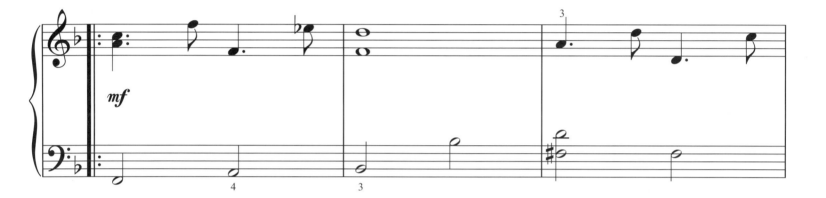

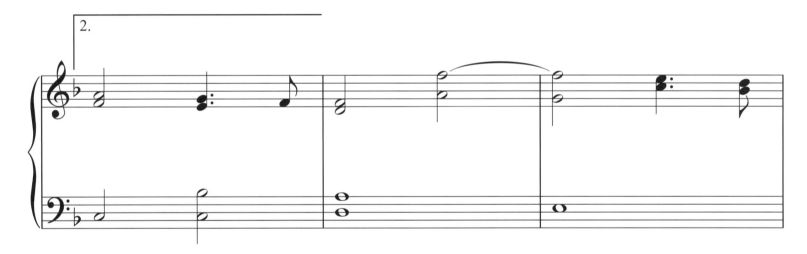

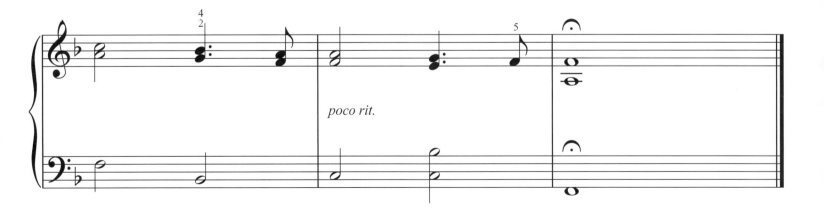

poco rit.

AIR IN D MINOR
from THE DOUBLE DEALER, Z. T676

By HENRY PURCELL
(1659–1695)

AIR
(Air on the G String)
from ORCHESTRAL SUITE NO. 3 IN D MAJOR, BWV 1068

By JOHANN SEBASTIAN BACH
(1685–1750)

Slowly

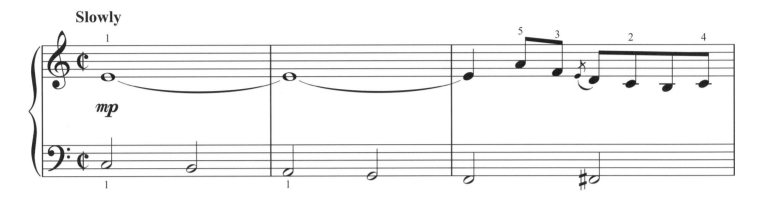

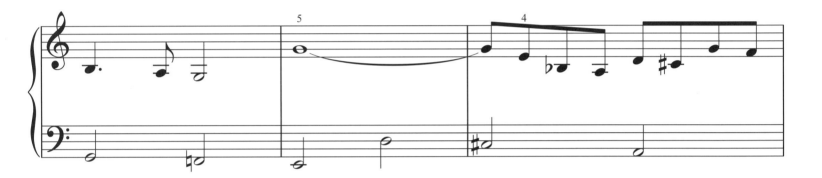

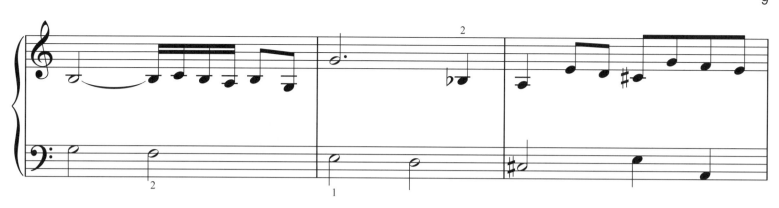

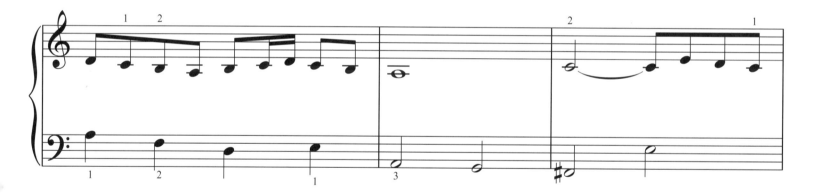

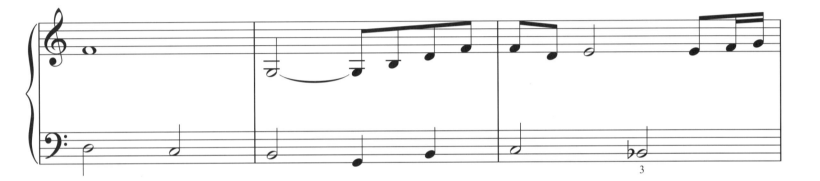

ALLEGRO MAESTOSO
from WATER MUSIC

By GEORGE FRIDERIC HANDEL
(1685–1759)

ARIA NO. 4

By GEORG PHILIPP TELEMANN
(1681–1767)

ARIOSO

By ALESSANDRO SCARLATTI
(1660–1725)

Adagio

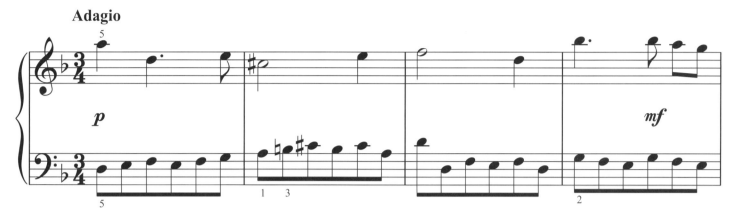

ARIOSO
from CANTATA NO. 156

By JOHANN SEBASTIAN BACH
(1685–1750)

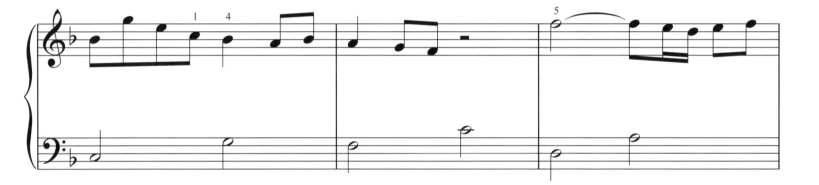

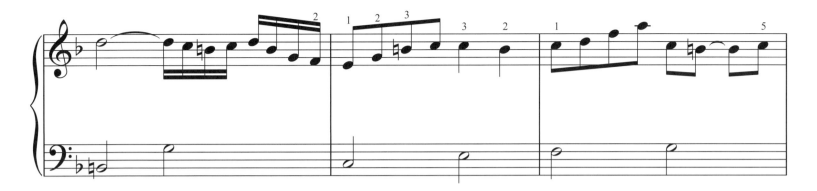

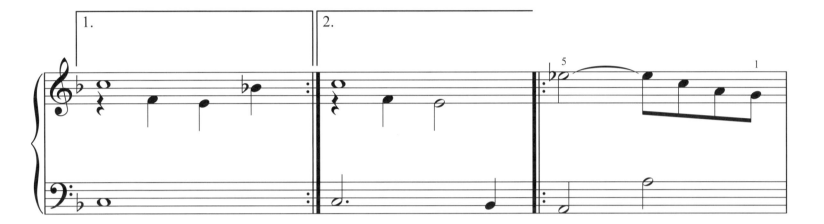

BADINERIE
(Suite No. 2)

By JOHANN SEBASTIAN BACH
(1685–1750)

Quickly, lightly

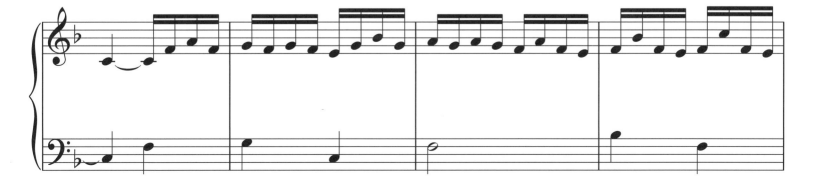

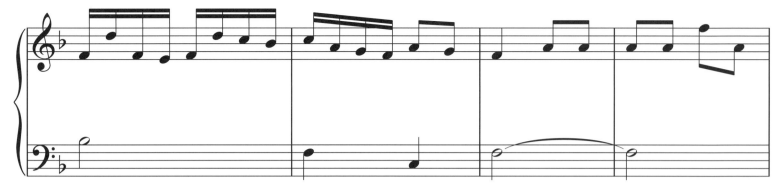

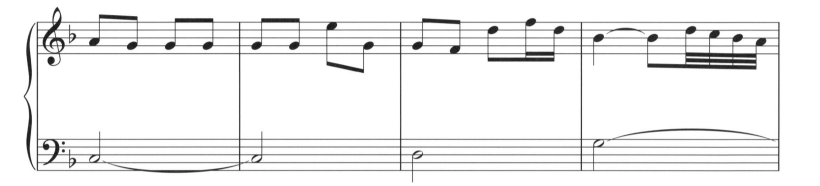

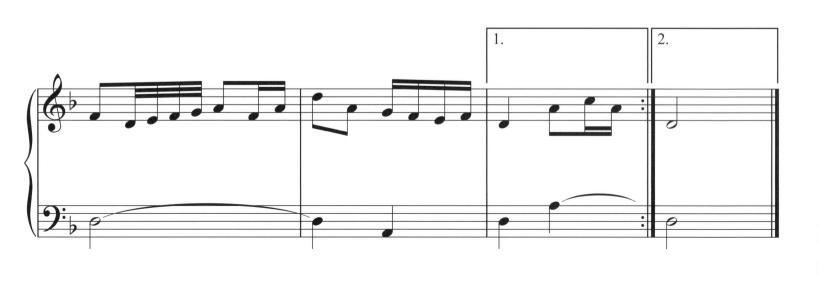

ARRIVAL OF THE QUEEN OF SHEBA

By GEORGE FRIDERIC HANDEL
(1685–1759)

Allegro

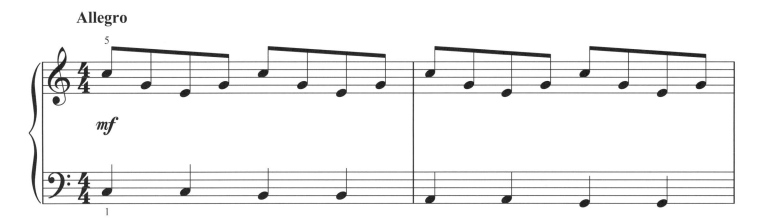

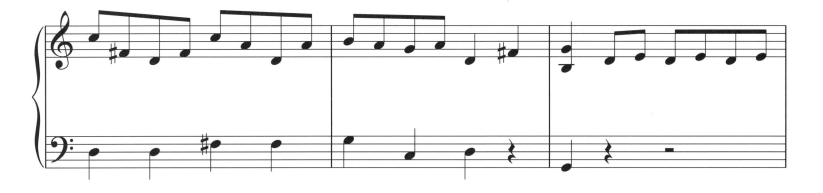

BIST DU BEI MIR

By GOTTFRIED HEINRICH STÖLZEL
(1690–1749)

Andante

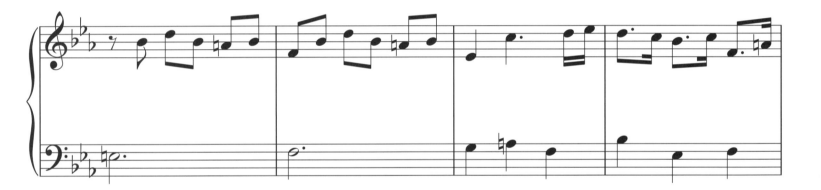

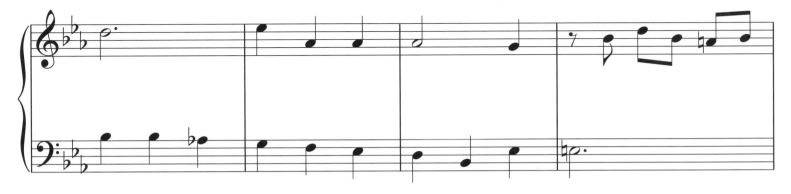

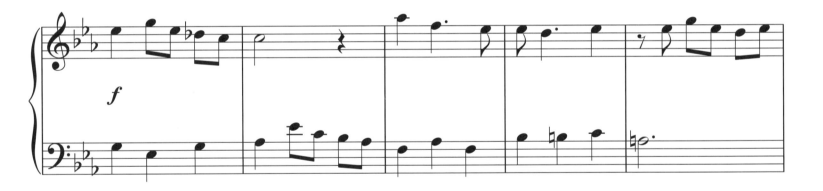

BOURÉE IN D MINOR

By CHRISTOPH GRAUPNER
(1683–1760)

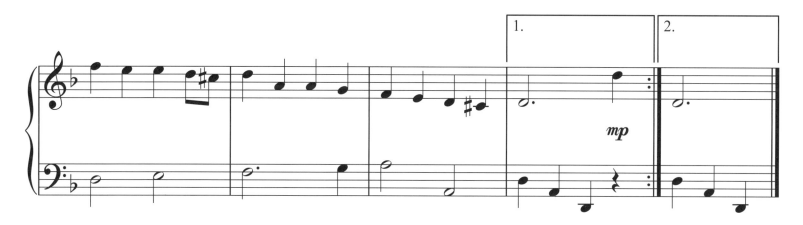

BOURÉE IN E MINOR

By JOHANN SEBASTIAN BACH
(1685–1750)

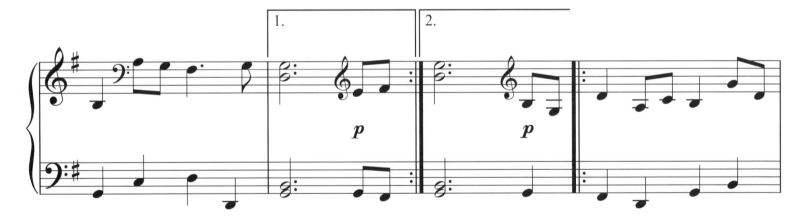

CANON IN D

By JOHANN PACHELBEL
(1653–1706)

Slowly

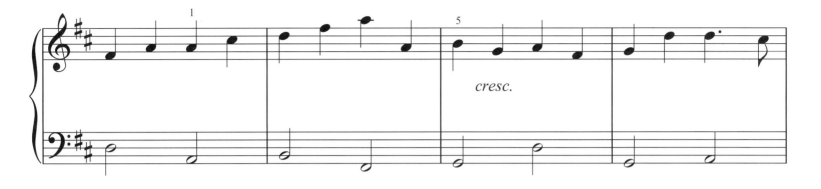

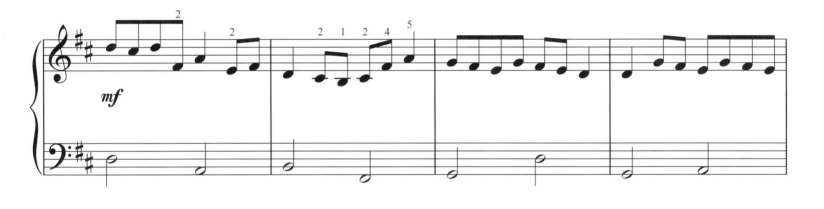

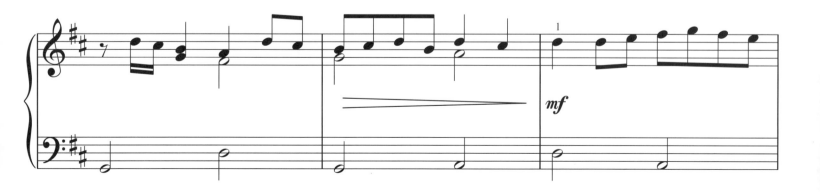

COURANTE

By GEORGE FRIDERIC HANDEL
(1685–1759)

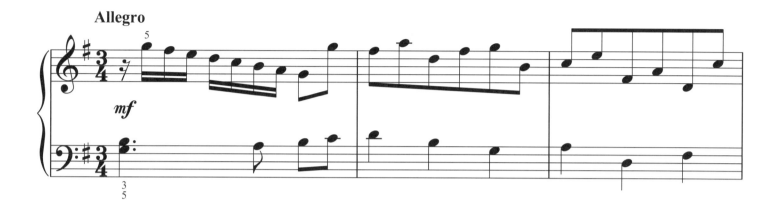

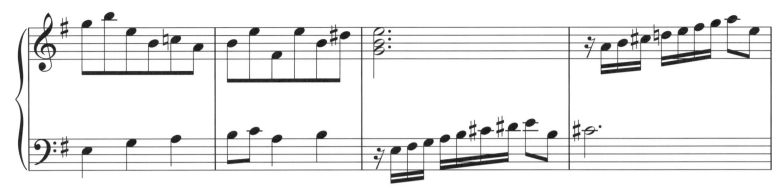

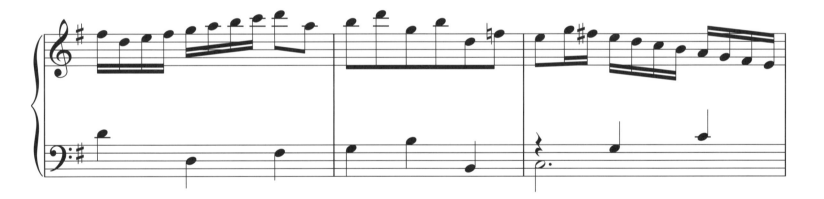

THE CUCKOO

By LOUIS-CLAUDE DAQUIN
(1694–1772)

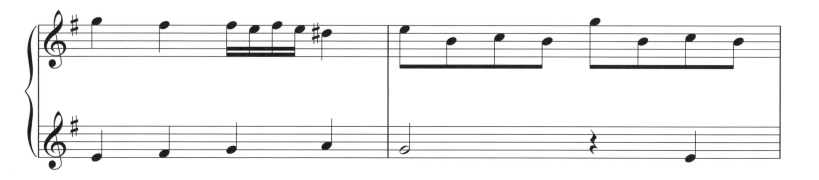

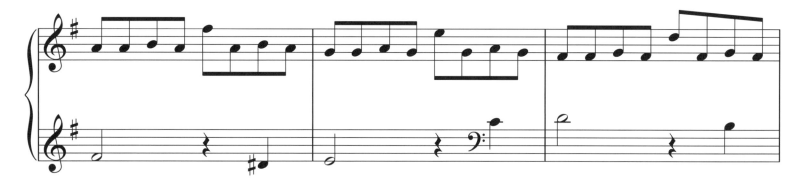

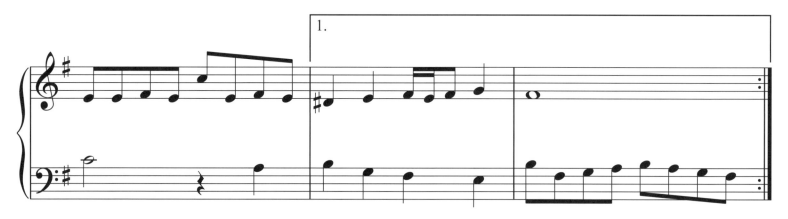

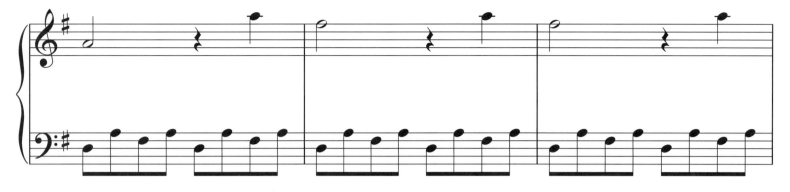

D.C. al Coda
(with repeats)

CODA

ECHO DANCE

By PHILIPP HAINHOFER
(1578–1647)

Moderato

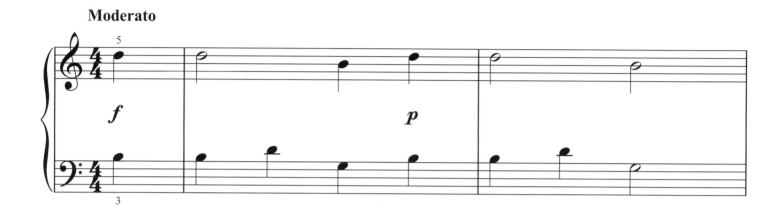

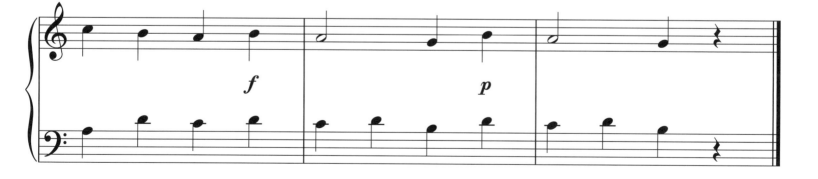

DANCE

By GEORG PHILIPP TELEMANN
(1681–1767)

Allegretto

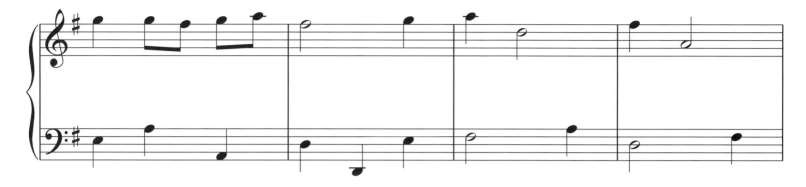

FANFARE RONDEAU

By JEAN-JOSEPH MOURET
(1682–1738)

Moderately

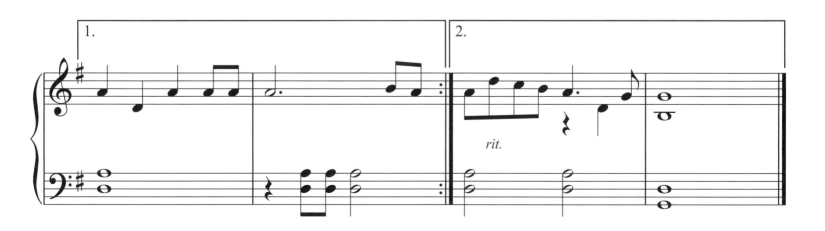

GAGLIARDA

By GIROLAMO FRESCOBALDI
(1583–1643)

Moderato

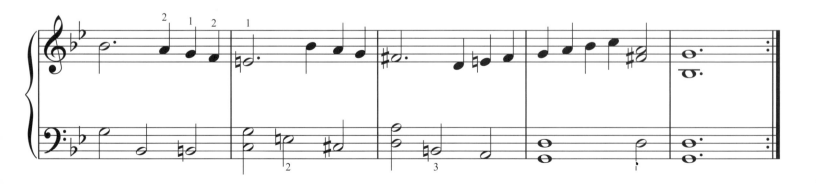

HARMONIOUS BLACKSMITH
(Theme)

By GEORGE FRIDERIC HANDEL
(1685–1759)

HORNPIPE
from WATER MUSIC

By GEORGE FRIDERIC HANDEL
(1685–1759)

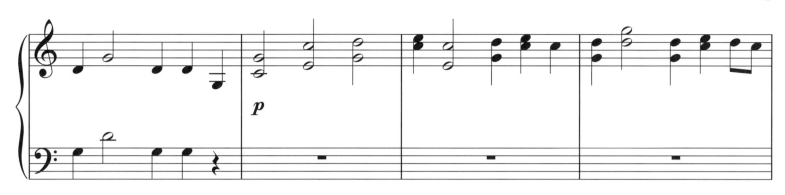

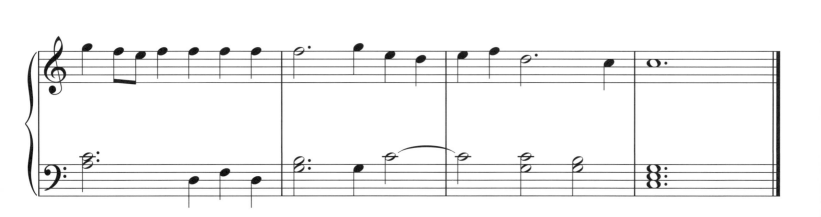

I KNOW THAT MY REDEEMER LIVETH
from MESSIAH

By GEORGE FRIDERIC HANDEL
(1685–1759)

52

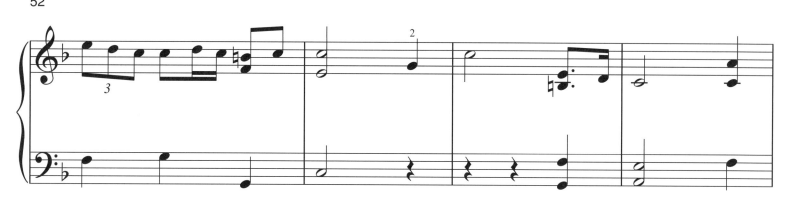

IMPERTINENCE
HWV 494

By GEORGE FRIDERIC HANDEL
(1685–1759)

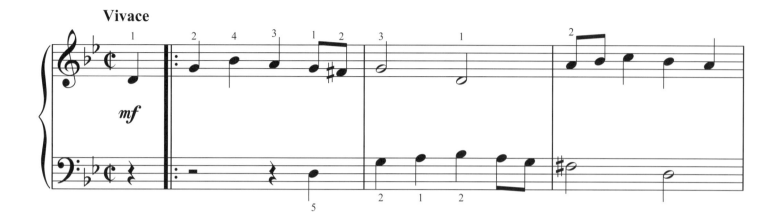

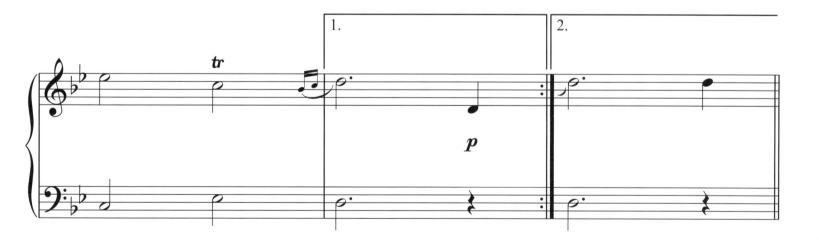

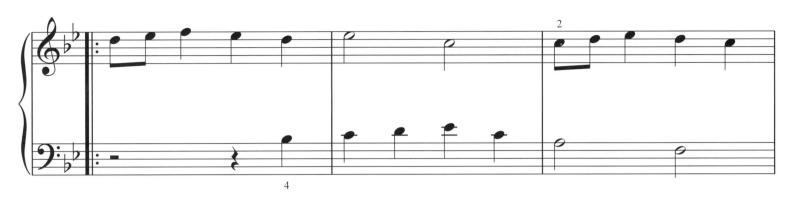

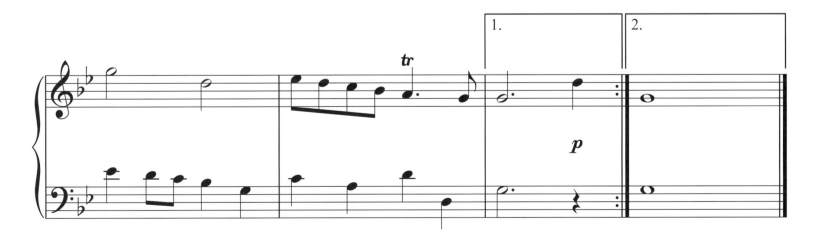

JESU, JOY OF MAN'S DESIRING

By JOHANN SEBASTIAN BACH
(1685–1750)

LARGO

By ARCANGELO CORELLI
(1653–1713)

LACHRIMAE ANTIQUAE

By JOHN DOWLAND
(1563–1626)

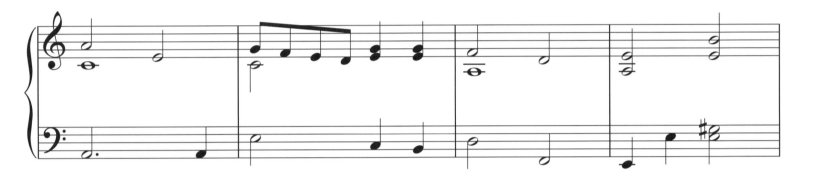

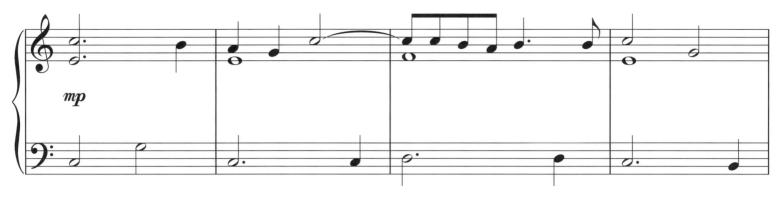

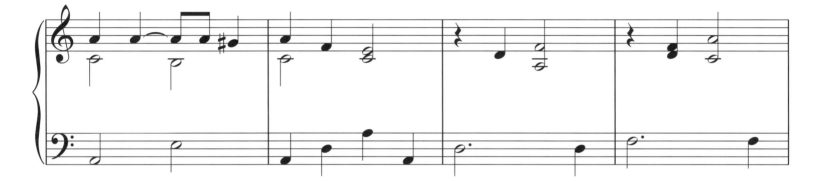

D.C. al Fine

LARGHETTO

By ALESSANDRO SCARLATTI
(1685–1757)

Larghetto

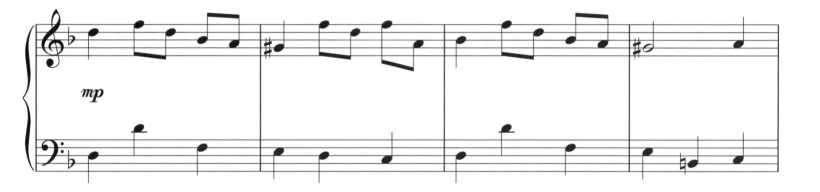

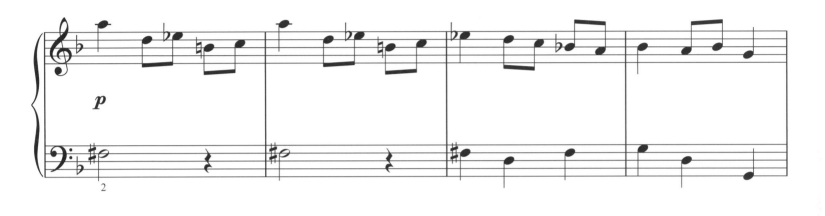

LITTLE PRELUDE NO. 2 IN C MAJOR

By JOHANN SEBASTIAN BACH
(1685–1750)

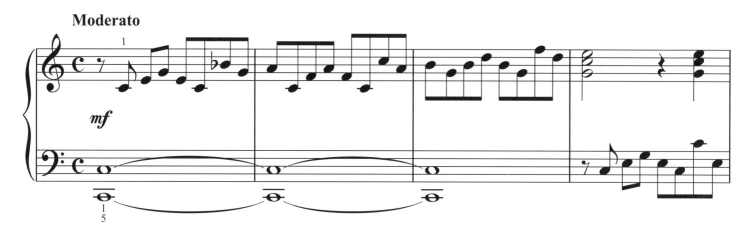

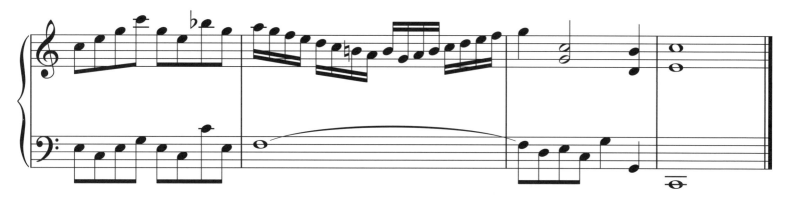

LULLABY IN F MAJOR

By JOHANN PHILIPP KIRNBERGER
(1721–1783)

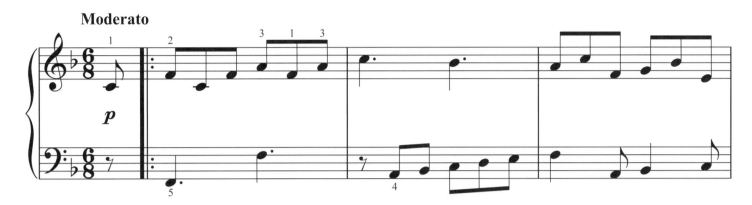

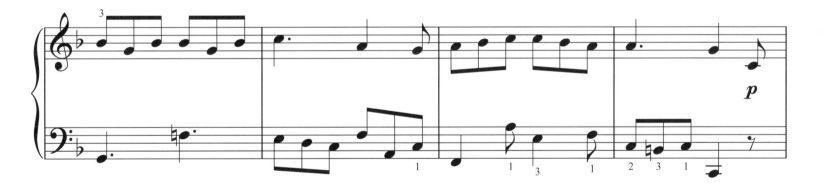

MARCH IN D MAJOR
from THE LITTLE CLAVIER BOOK FOR ANNA MAGDALENA BACH

By JOHANN SEBASTIAN BACH
(1685–1750)

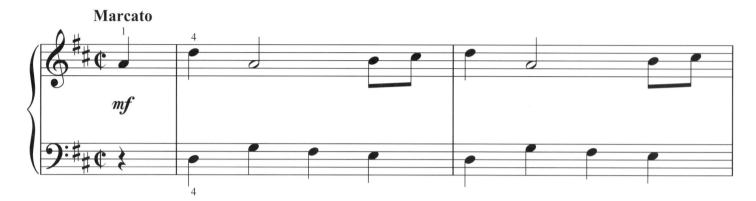

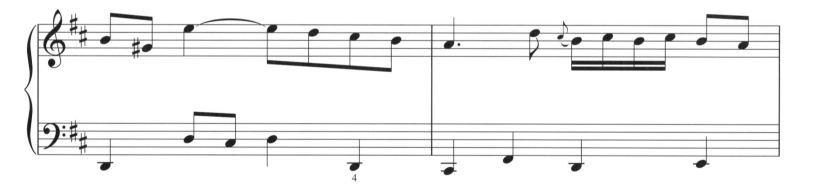

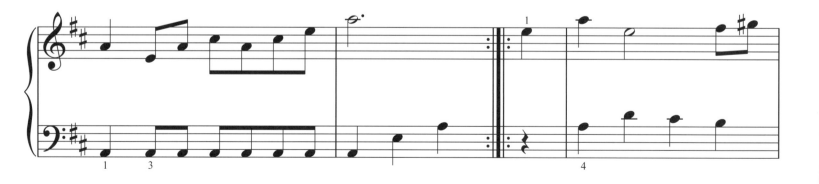

MENUET EN RONDEAU

By JEAN-PHILLIPE RAMEAU
(1683–1764)

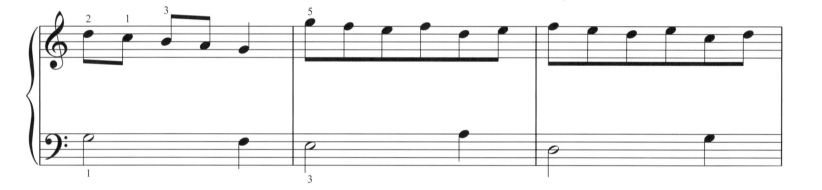

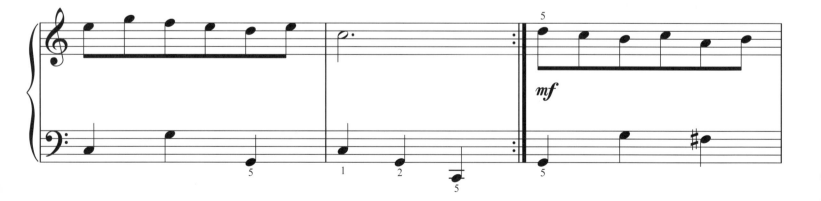

MENUET IN D MINOR
BWV App. 132

Composer Unknown
18th century

Andante

MENUET IN G MAJOR
BWV App. 114

By CHRISTIAN PETZOLD
(1677–1733)

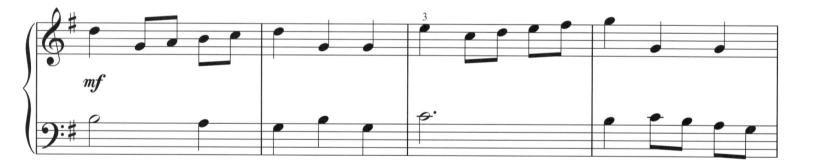

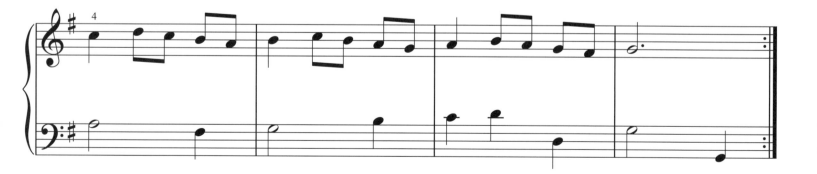

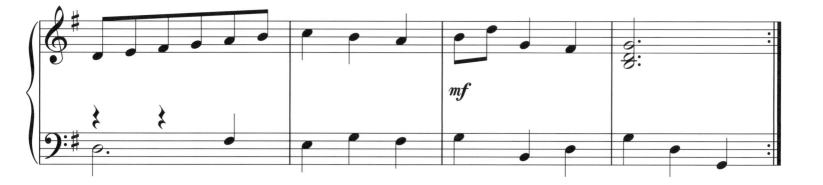

MENUET IN G MAJOR
BWV App. 116

Composer Unknown
18th century

Moderato

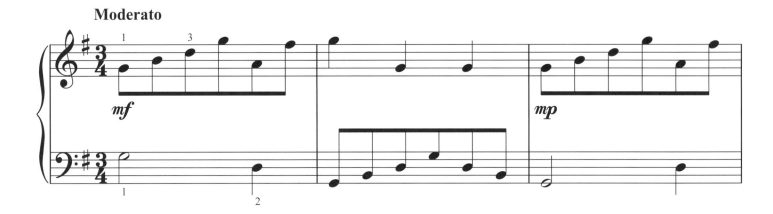

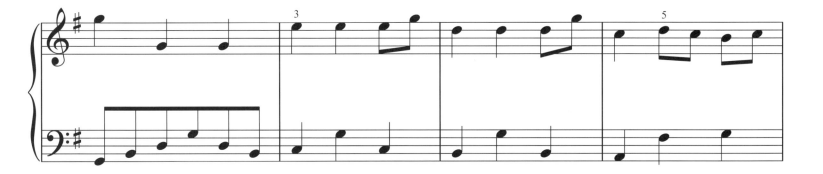

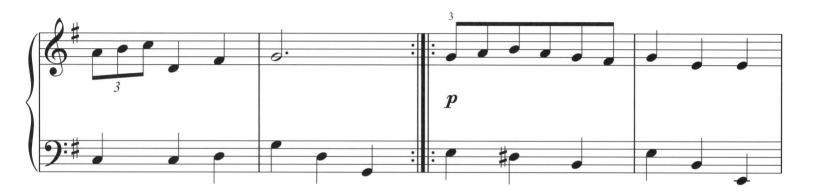

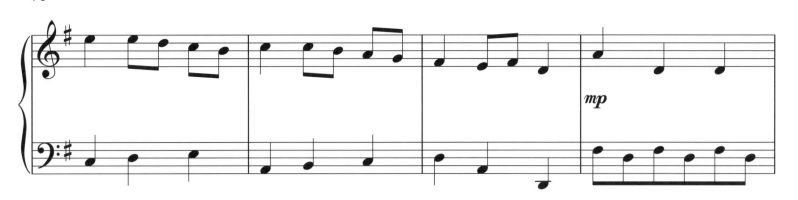

MINUET IN A MINOR

By JOHANN KRIEGER
(1651–1735)

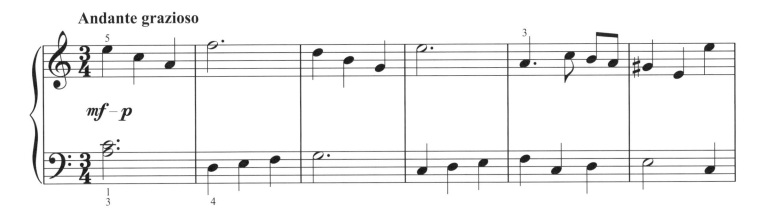

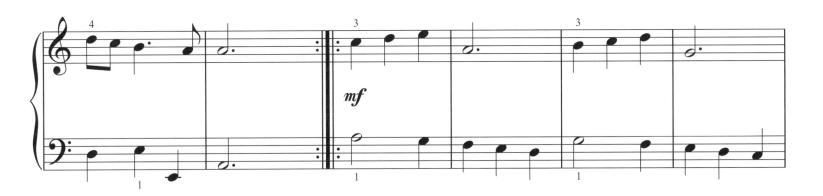

MINUET IN G MAJOR

By JOHANN SEBASTIAN BACH
(1685–1750)

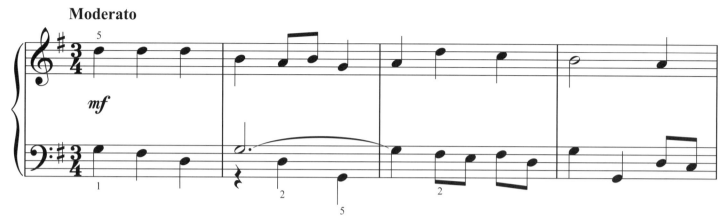

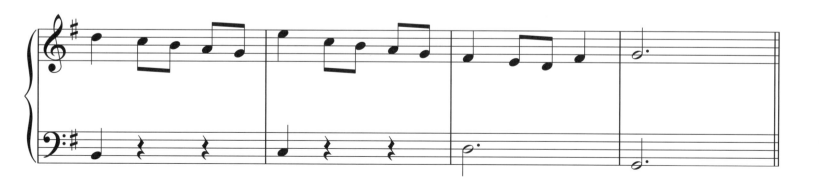

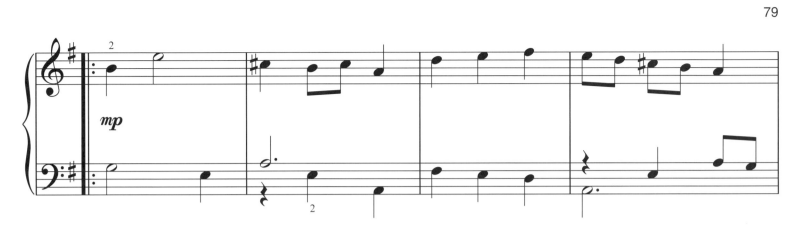

MINUET IN G MAJOR

By GEORG PHILIPP TELEMANN
(1681–1767)

Moderato

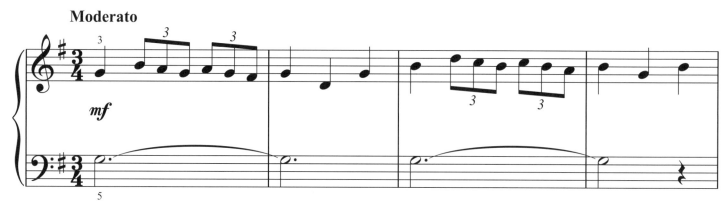

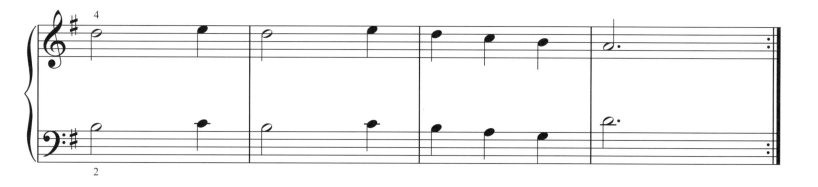

PASSEPIED IN C MAJOR

HWV 559

By GEORGE FRIDERIC HANDEL
(1685–1759)

Con spirito

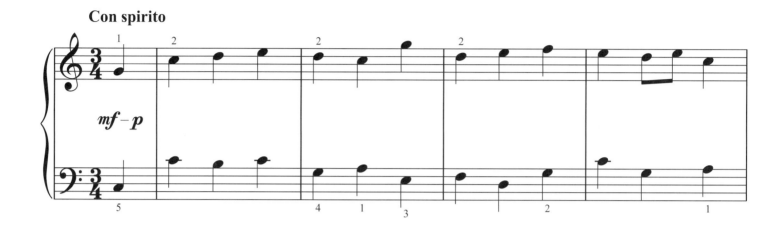

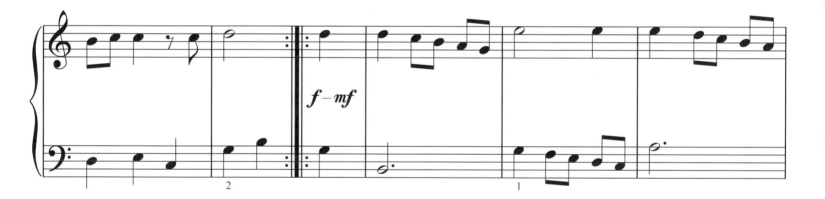

MUSETTE IN D MAJOR
from THE LITTLE CLAVIER BOOK FOR ANNA MAGDALENA BACH

By JOHANN SEBASTIAN BACH
(1685–1750)

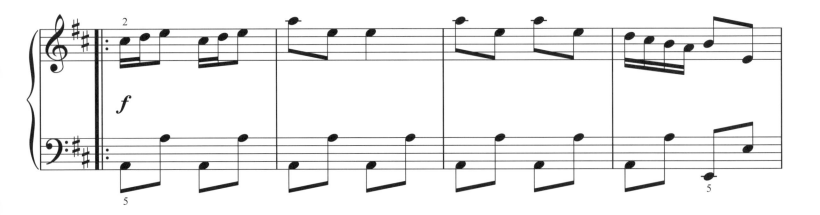

SARABANDA

By ARCANGELO CORELLI
(1653–1713)

Expressively

SARABANDE

By GEORGE FRIDERIC HANDEL
(1685–1759)

Larghetto

SHEEP MAY SAFELY GRAZE
from CANTATA BWV 208

By JOHANN SEBASTIAN BACH
(1685–1750)

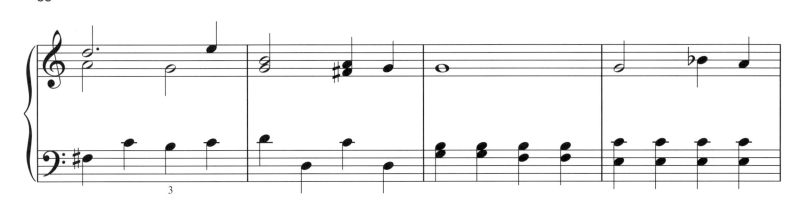

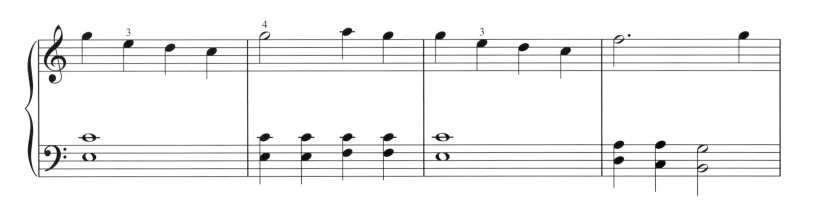

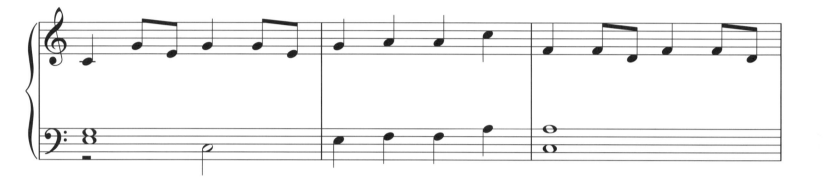

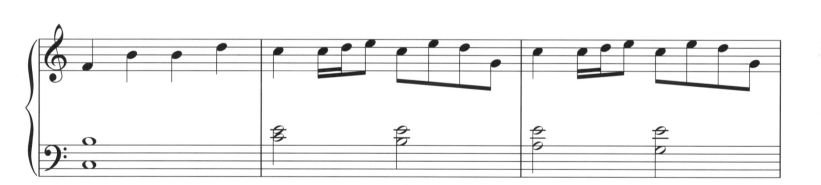

SOLFEGGIO

By JOHANN CHRISTOPH FRIEDRICH BACH
(1732–1795)

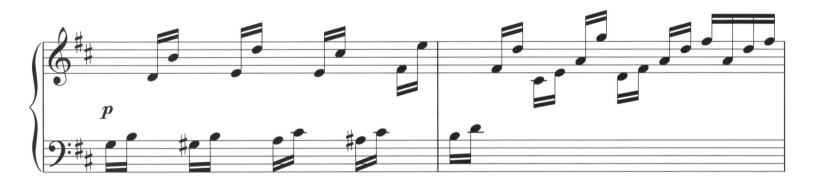

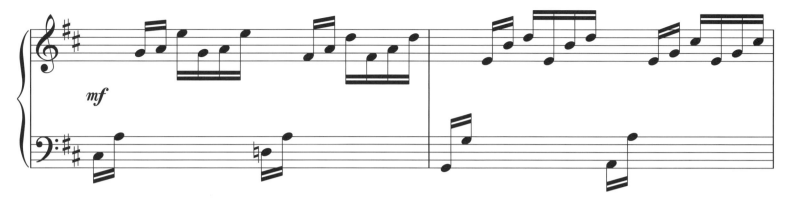

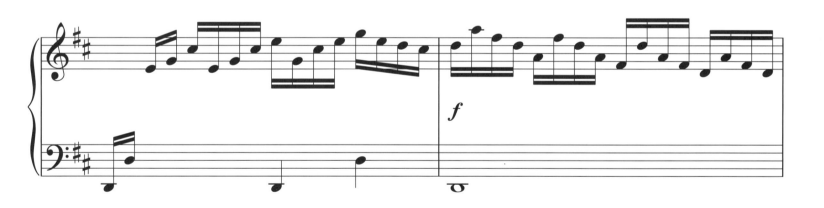

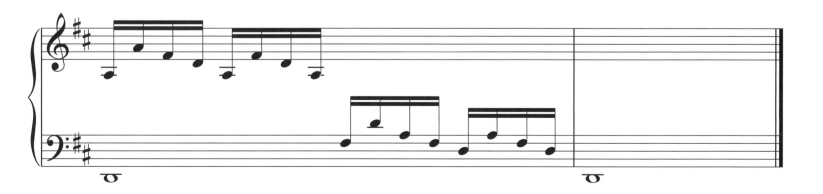

SONATA IN A MAJOR
L. 483

By DOMENICO SCARLATTI
(1685–1757)

Allegro

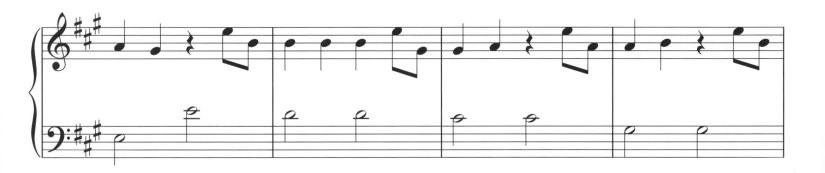

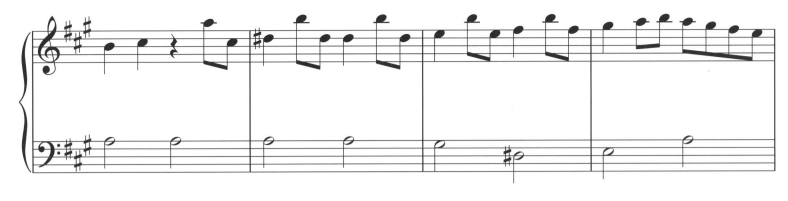

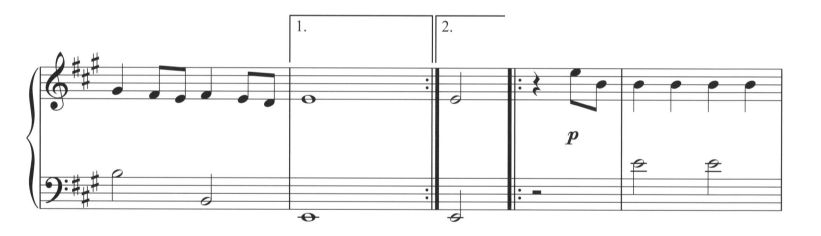

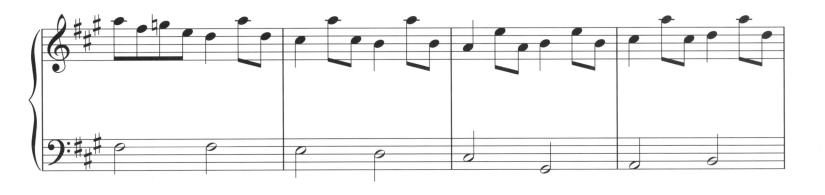

SONATINA

By WILLIAM DUNCOMBE
(1690–1769)

Allegretto

SONATA IN C MAJOR
L. 217

By DOMENICO SCARLATTI
(1685–1757)

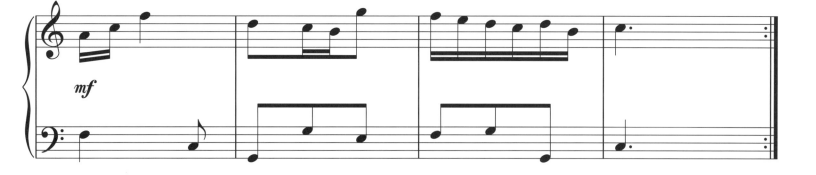

TRUMPET TUNE

By WILLIAM DUNCOMBE
(ca. 1736–ca. 1818)

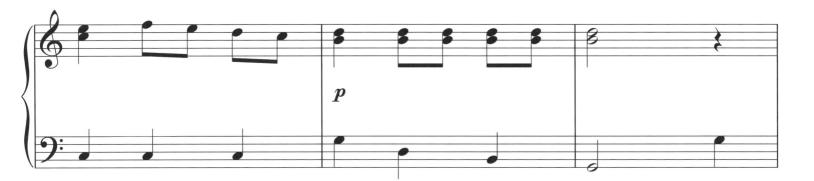

TRUMPET TUNE

By HENRY PURCELL
(1659–1695)

Moderately

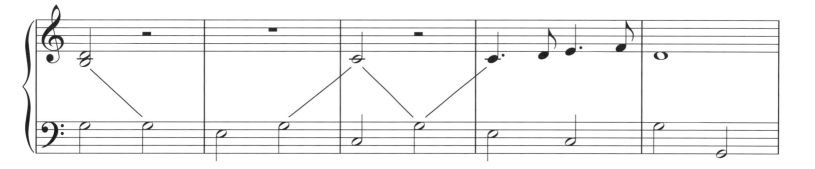

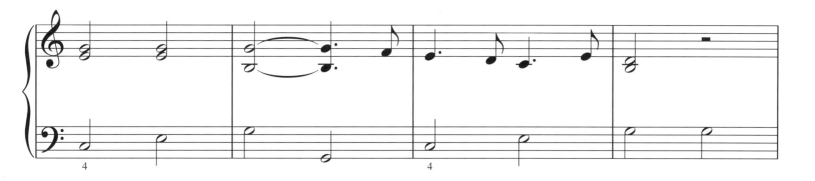

SPRING
from THE FOUR SEASONS

By ANTONIO VIVALDI
(1678–1741)

Moderately